WAR NO LONGER EXISTS

General Rupert Smith's 2008 book, *"The Utility of War"*[1], presents an excellent insight into the nature and conduct of war in the twenty-first century. Smith draws upon a wealth of practical experience and lessons learned during 40 years of military service and argues that a paradigm shift has occurred in warfare changing why and how military force is applied in the world today and who wields it.

Smith wrote, "[w]ar no longer exists…war as battle in a field between men and machinery, war as a massive deciding event in a dispute in international affairs: such war no longer exists"[2] Although intra- and interstate conflicts will continue to exist, how they are fought and resolved has changed, thus creating a new paradigm. States are no longer the primary actors in conflicts. Non-state actors, including warlords, tribes, guerillas/insurgent groups, narco-terrorists and religious extremist groups are responsible for the preeminence of intrastate conflicts today. With very few exceptions, countries will not conduct interstate industrial wars seeking a decisive victory in order to achieve conflict resolution. Interstate wars are increasingly rare today and are vastly different than the great wars of Napoleon or WWII. That said, Smith wrote in 2007 that NATO nations, Russia, most former Soviet states and many other nations are "…organized to fight industrial wars whilst engaged in war amongst the people."[3] Smith further argues that civilian casualties and displacement are no longer incidental to the conduct of war, but are frequently an objective of the conflict.

This essay will first critically examine Smith's assertion of a paradigm shift in war using research studies on international conflict, and the level of acceptance of this paradigm as reflected in the national strategic policy documents of the U.S., U.K.,

Australia, and Germany as well as Russia and China. Second, it will question if America's military, as it is now organized and equipped, reflects its emerging, "Smithian" National Security Policy. Third, it will present some thoughts on the strategic way ahead in this time of increasingly constrained military budgets and ambiguous and constantly-shifting national threats.

Theoretical Underpinnings and Supporting Data of Smith's Thesis

Smith does not claim to be a strategic theorist, nor was the purpose of his book to introduce a new theory of war. Instead, he freely characterizes the book as a product of personal reflection, "…not a work of definitive research" and more of a "…thematic discussion rather than a definitive history…"[4] As such, the book lacks any references to academic studies of warfare or corroborating theorists (this is unfortunate since the preponderance of research clearly documents the decline of interstate war in the 20th and 21st centuries)[5].

Smith cleverly intertwines history, recent personal experiences, and the challenges of modern conflicts to convince readers of his thesis. General Smith's forty years of military service, often commanding at the most senior levels, provide a wealth of experience to draw upon. He commanded a British Armored Division in the 1991 Gulf War, UN Forces in Bosnia in 1995, British Forces in Northern Ireland from 1996-98, and finally as the NATO Deputy Supreme Allied Commander from 1998-2001.

As a result of this command experience, Smith offers a compelling argument of a paradigm shift between the advent of the atomic age and the face of war in the twenty-first century due to the following six major trends:

1. The ends for which we are fighting are changing to objectives having to do with individuals and societies that are not states.

2. The tools of industrial wars are often irrelevant to war amongst people.

3. Conflicts seek a condition that may take years or decades to accomplish.

4. We fight so as not to lose the force rather than fighting to achieve the aim.

5. We tend to conduct conflicts in multinational groupings.

6. We fight amongst people – in the living room and in the streets.[6]

The Demise of Interstate War

Smith begins his book with the contentious and thought-provoking statement that war no longer exists. However, he quickly caveats this statement in order to reconcile it with the existence of crises and conflicts throughout the world. Smith argues that states no longer conduct wars mobilizing their populations and industries to create a massive, technologically advanced, military force that seeks a decisive victory in a battle or series of battles typical of the Napoleonic Wars or WWII. Unfortunately, Smith's book suffers contextually by not clearly defining what industrial war is, despite this being a central point of his argument. Smith draws on his experiences in Bosnia and Desert Storm to describe the transformation in international politics where wars are no longer declared, but simply fought. Nations "intervene" based on international resolutions authorizing the use of force. Conflicts now have ambiguous ends such as ceasefires or agreements rather than peace treaties. Examples include: the March 1991 Gulf War ceasefire between America and Iraq, Eritrea and Ethipias ceasefire in 2000 ending a two year war resulting in 70,000 casualties, and the August 2008 ceasefire ending a brief war between Georgia and Russia.

Smith's central thesis is that warfare today rarely involves two states, as it did in Westphalian times. Instead, wars are fought between governments and terrorists, warlords, separatists, and in and among nations' populations. Mary Kaldor echoes this view, arguing that states are no longer the primary actors in war.[7] Martin van Creveld agrees, writing that Clausewitz's definition of war as being between two states is obsolete due to the rise of nonstate warfare in recent times.[8] Even Edward Newman, in an article critical of Rupert Smith's book, acknowledged that despite a minor rise in interstate wars in the mid-1990s "…civil war has been more frequent than interstate war."[9] Finally, Kalevi Holsti's analysis of worldwide conflict found the rate of interstate wars dropped seven-fold between 1941 and 1995, despite a four-fold increase in the number of states (from 30 to 140).[10]

But Smith's opening statement begs the issue: has there actually been a decrease in interstate wars? The preponderance of studies indicate that since 1946 intrastate war superseded international war as the primary form of conflict throughout the world.[11] Yet the utmost caution must be exercised when using results from multiple studies since definitions and parameters vary significantly between research centers and study authors.

Superficial comparisons of study results can lead to erroneous conclusions since study parameters are often significantly different. Examples include: not including all countries, dismissing conflicts because of insignificant casualties, or how a particular study categorizes a conflict. Many studies exclude countries with less than 500,000 inhabitants and thus only examine approximately 162 countries (the U.S. State Department recognizes 194). Other studies vary on whether they categorize approximately 19 post-WWII wars of colonialism and liberation as being interstate, intrastate, or "extrastate.[12]

Also, particular attention must be paid to the terms, and the definition of those terms, used by each study and researcher before one can understand the study and begin to make useful comparisons with other studies. Even the common verbiage of "conflict", "crisis" and "war" can have very specific and dissimilar meanings for various studies, particularly when classification thresholds rely on casualty figures. For instance, the Human Security Report Project and the Center for Systemic Peace (CSP) define conflicts using casualty thresholds. The Human Security Report Project defines a conflict as having 25 to 1,000 battle related casualties a year, and beyond 1,000 it becomes a war.[13] The Center for Systemic Peace only reports "major conflicts" which it defines as 500 "directly-related" fatalities and a sustained rate of 100 casualties per annum."[14] However, "[t]he Heidelberg Institute on International Conflict Research (HIIK) defines conflict "…as the clashing of interests (positional differences) over national values of some duration and magnitude between two parties…"[15]

Furthermore, instead of body counts, HIIK uses a "…qualitative definition of conflict and war. Wars and conflicts of lesser intensity are classified according to the actual amount of violence observed, and not according to the number of fatalities."[16] HIIK then subcategorizes conflicts by their state of violence and level of intensity before finally "naming" them. From least to most violent they are 1) non-violent or latent conflict, 2) violent or manifest conflict, 3) crisis; a conflict with sporadic violent incidents, 4) severe crisis; severely violent and 5) war. All categories can be characterized as either inter- or intrastate.[17] But simply categorizing conflicts as either inter- or intrastate often fails to provide an accurate understanding of the conflict's true nature as demonstrated by the brief, five day Russia-Georgian War in 2008, which both the HIIK,[18] and Center for Systemic Peace[19] listed as an interstate conflict. Although the Georgian regions of Abkhaz and South Ossetia were semi-autonomous, significant portions of their populations desired to be part of Russia. The political status of these regions was further complicated after 2002 when Russia began recognizing South Ossetians as Russian citizens and began issuing tens of thousands of passports.[20] Once fighting commenced, Russia and Georgia fought using regular forces operating as battalions and brigades, employing artillery, seaborne landings, and close air support from helicopters and jets under the command of their respective national commands. However, Russia also armed and employed local militia units as well as paramilitary forces, including Cossack volunteers who assisted in ethnically cleansing Georgians from the breakaway provinces.[21]

The Dominance of Intrastate War

Despite the discrepancies among study methodologies, the preponderance of analyses indicate the current dominance of intrastate wars is the result of a continuous evolution of war since 1945. Kalevi Holsti's study of conflicts from 1945-1995 found that "[a]lmost 77 percent of the 164 wars were internal, where armed conflict was not against the state but against authorities within the state or between armed communities."[22] Gurr, Marshall and Khosla, from the Center for International Development and Conflict Management (CIDCM), found "[s]ocietal conflict was roughly three times the magnitude of interstate war during most of the last half of the [20th] century and increased six-fold between the 1950s and the early 1990s.[23] The 2009 annual "Conflict Barometer" study by the HIIK found an overwhelming majority of high intensity conflicts (defined as highly violent crisis or war) occurring between 1975 and 2009 were intrastate. In fact, all of the 31 highly-violent conflicts, and 106 of 112 crises (defined as sporadically violent

6

conflicts) were intrastate. Furthermore, the annual average of interstate conflicts was 35 compared to just three interstate events.[24]

Particularly since 2000, the demise of interstate conflict is striking, averaging just one a year since.[25] CIDCM found that in the last ten years, the number of new conflicts has been quite low, never exceeding three in a given year. Since 2000, there have been five years with no new conflicts at all. No decade since the end of World War II has witnessed so many years in which no newly triggered conflicts have been added to the roster of active conflict. [26]

But is this trend irreversible? If not, how long will the trend continue? The short answer is that no one knows and prediction of future behaviors is fraught with risk. Sources of current and future conflicts include: scarcity of water, natural resources in contested territorial areas, poverty, proliferation and rise of local warlords, ethnic strife, insurgent groups operating in neighboring territories, a growing international economic divide, and international intervention for humanitarian reasons. However, none of these issues or tensions predetermine war as the inevitable outcome. The international community has grappled with each of them for decades and, at least since the Second World War, has generally been able to find peaceful resolutions in the end. However, these international efforts have varying degrees of "success." Nigeria's withdrawl from Cameroon's oil rich Bakassi Peninsula after the International Criminal Court ruled in Cameroon's favor, was completely peaceful. A less successful effort is the United nations peacekeeping in Sudan's Darfur region where conflict and violence continue. Finally, the political solution in Cyprus remains in limbo as the 1964 ceasefire between Greece and Turkey remains. These efforts though there are numerous examples of this capacity for peaceful conflict resolution should continue to increase as more nations adopt democratic governmental institutions and mature in their use. Erica Frantz, from the Center for International Development and Conflict Management, found the risk of coups and internal or external wars was roughly three to four times higher in autocracies and anocracies (hybrid states exhibiting characteristics of both democracies and autocracies) than democracies. [27]

According to most scholars, the rise of stable democracies (those lasting ten years or longer) is one of the main reasons for the overall reduction of inter- and intrastate wars. Stable democracies have a greater institutional capability to receive, integrate and enact legislation to correct grievances and injustices and deal with climatic changes, thereby preventing escalation of intrastate tensions. Democracy also allows populations the opportunity to elect officials who will represent their views and peacefully resolve external conflicts. In 1978 autocracies outnumbered democracies more than two-to-one. By 1992 there were 78 democracies and 40 autocracies;[28] by 2007 there were 94 democracies.[29]

International intervention, often for humanitarian reasons, also occurs in increasing frequency and effectiveness. Political bodies such as the UN, European Union (EU), NATO and the African Union (AU), are deploying an ever-increasing number of peacekeepers to trouble spots in order to diffuse or prevent escalation of inter- or intrastate conflicts. Examples include: UN missions in Israel, Cyprus and Western Sahara; EU forces in Kosovo and Chad; and the AU in South Sudan and Somalia. Intrastate wars destabilize regions and have the potential of escalating into an interstate war. For example, decades of conflict in the Democratic Republic of Congo were initiated by multiple armed groups operating from, or supported by, portions of five neighboring states.[30] Intrastate violence thus risks spilling over into neighboring countries through cross-border raids or air strikes by government forces aiming at fleeing groups or safe havens. As a result, in November 2011, the U.S. and AU separately committed military forces to combat one of these groups, the Lord's Resistance Army (LRA). The LRA currently operates in Uganda, Sudan, the Democratic Republic of Congo, and the Central African Republic and has moved easily between these nations since its creation in 1987.

Various Examples of Current National Security Policies and Strategy

Recent American and other nations' national security policies and planning doctrine reflect an overall acceptance of Rupert Smith's paradigm shift from conventional wars between nations to operations in a wide variety of enduring and emerging intrastate conflicts. The U.S. 2010 Quadrennial Defense Review recognized this change of paradigms, finding "…it is no longer appropriate to speak of "major regional conflicts" as the sole or even the primary template for sizing, shaping, and evaluating U.S. forces."[31] America's 2009 Joint Doctrine for the Armed Forces of the United States claims, "Irregular warfare (IW) has emerged as a major and pervasive form of warfare."[32] This publication further expounds on the dilemma facing the United States of whether to prepare for the least likely scenario of a major war against a military power, or to build forces for "forms of war [that] are all but guaranteed…but don't pose the same existential threat."[33]

Recently U.S. military doctrine began using the term "hybrid" threats when describing wars and national security threats in recognition of the complexity and variety of threats and actors in world conflict. Leaders sought to capture insights learned

9

through years of intense operational experience in Iraq, Afghanistan, Philippines and Yemen, and create a more accurate and useful common operational terminology. Army doctrine defines "[a] hybrid threat is the diverse and dynamic combination of regular forces, irregular forces, terrorist forces, criminal elements, or a combination of these forces and elements all unified to achieve mutually benefitting effects."[34] Also, hybrid threats may involve nation state or non-nation state actors. Although the term hybrid is intentionally broad, elastic, and inclusive, U.S. doctrine has evolved and shares General Smith's view that the focus of modern warfare and security is no longer interstate wars. However, as will be discussed later , America's procurement programs and force composition does not mirror this evolution in national defense policy. Instead, America will increase its procurement of advanced fighter aircraft   an area of significant conventional over-capacity — while reducing Army and Marine ground personnel. As a result, in 2012, General Dempsey, the U.S. Chairman of the Joint Chiefs of Staff, testified America's armed forces "...will no longer be sized for large scale, prolonged stability operations."[35]

The national strategic policies and doctrines of the U.K., Australia, South Africa Germany, and China echo General Smith's belief in the primacy of non-state actors and intrastate conflict in today's operating environment. On the other hand, Russia expresses a more comprehensive but xenophobic view, perceiving threats from NATO, separatist movements, terrorists, and cyber activities.

The United Kingdom's 2010 National Security Strategy provides a historical background to today's environment, describing the transition from the existential threat posed by the Soviet Union and the Warsaw Pact to today's myriad complex threats, including terrorism, cyber attack, and unconventional attacks using nuclear, biological of chemical weapons.[36] The U.K.'s top defense priorities are protecting counter-terrorism capabilities to defeat terrorism, particularly from Al Qaeda and terrorist groups linked to Northern Ireland,[37] as well as cyber security program development."[38] As a result, the entire British Army of the Northern Rhine, some 20,000 troops, will be permanently redeployed from Germany by 2015. Furthermore, the severe budget cuts of 2010-2015, imposed by the Ministry of Defense, prioritize resources by cutting conventional weapons in all sectors except Special Forces, which will receive additional equipment for combating terrorism. [39] Cuts include eliminating 100 tanks, cancelling the Harrier aircraft – its only naval aircraft capability – reducing naval surface combatants from 24 to 19, and cutting an armored brigade. Cuts will continue beyond 2015 when one of the two newly built Queen Elizabeth-class carriers is mothballed in 2019, after just three years of operation.[40]

Australia's 2009 Defense White Paper presents a very thorough discussion of threats to its national security, the resultant strategies and resource prioritization, and explains the risks accepted by Australia's strategy out to 2030. The White Paper finds the likelihood of foreign military forces attacking in sufficient strength to threaten Australia's national way of life as currently very remote, and did not identify any country or groups of countries which would pose such a threat. [41] Furthermore, Australian leaders mirror Smith's view that intrastate conflict will "…be an enduring feature, and the most common form, in the period to 2030…" However, they wrote "…it would be premature to judge that war among states, including the major powers, has been eliminated as a feature of the international system."[42]

11

Unfortunately, the Australian government adopted a force strategy totally inconsistent with the security threats presented in the white paper. The government adopted a "strategic hedging" policy: balancing capabilities while maintaining an intellectual flexibility to critically re-examine existing capabilities and re-balance as needed due to uncertainty and unpredictable future world events. As a result, the main role of Australian Defense Forces continues to be "…an ability to engage in conventional combat against other armed forces…[and]…on developing a force that meets the primary obligation to deter and defeat attacks on Australia."[43] In order to accomplish this, Australia chose a defense policy essentially founded on a maritime strategy of sea control and air superiority. Australia's future procurement priorities are 12 submarines, three Air Warfare Destroyers, eight frigates, 24 naval combat helicopters, and 100 Joint Strike Fighters.[44]

South Africa's 2008 Defense White Paper claimed the long term future cannot be determined with any degree of certainty. But since the end of the Cold War "[t]he vast majority of armed conflicts are taking place within, rather than between states."[45] As a result, South Africa prioritized its defense budget on personnel wages, training and living conditions while cutting naval sea days and Air Force flight hours (each Gripen Fighter pilot will only fly 10 hours in 2011).[46]

Germany's 2011 Defense Policy Guidelines states that "[a] direct territorial threat to Germany involving conventional military means remains an unlikely event…Today, risks and threats are emerging above all from failing and failed states, acts of international terrorism, terrorist regimes and dictatorships…"[47] Germany's 2006 Defense White Paper echoes America's concept of hybrid war describing security challenges as "...new and ever more complex ..." and mentioned conflicts within states and WMD proliferation but found international terrorism "...the most immediate danger to security perpetrated methodically in transnational networks." [48] The first function listed for Germany's military is "international conflict prevention and crisis management, to include the fight against international terrorism."[49] As a result, Germany is transforming the majority of its Army into "stabilization forces." Stabilization forces are capable of operating in low to mid-intensity multinational operations, and will outnumber "responsive" forces capable of high-intensity operations by two-to-one (or 70,000 and 35,000 respectively).[50]

China views "[t]he Asia-Pacific security situation [as] generally stable" and describes the international security situation as "complex" pointing to rising terrorism, nuclear proliferation, and cyber insecurity. [51] China's defense expenditures are projected to continue growing at approximately 18 percent a year to 1) improve military personnel wages and living conditions, 2) improving military operations other than war (non-traditional security threats, counter-terrorism, humanitarian, and disaster relief) and, 3) moderately increased funds for high-tech weaponry. [52] China seeks to increase its national power through economic rather than military means. Chinese acquisition of modern weapons is appropriate and no different than other economic powerhouses such as Brazil or India. However, several countries, including the U.S., pointed to China's recent acquisition of an aircraft carrier from Russia, as a threat to regional stability. This embellishment of China's carrier capabilities is extremely misleading and self-serving. First, China is the only member of the India has operated a similar sized carrier for decades and intends to receive two more in the next six years. China's new carrier is half the size one of America's eleven carriers and can only operate 29 fixed wing aircraft – hardly a regional threat.

Finally, the 2010 Military Doctrine of Russia portrays a country facing numerous external and internal security threats. "Main external threats of war" come from NATO (listed first), foreign military contingents in territories bordering Russia, territorial claims against Russia, WMD proliferation, and international terrorism. The main internal military threat is "the, violation of the unity and territorial integrity of [the Russian Federation]."[53]

However, attempting to draw any useful correlations between Russia's military doctrine, spending, and force structure is perilous due to hidden spending (subsidies to industries) deliberate inaccuracies, unsupportable political promises, and fraud (up to 20 percent of defense spending is stolen).[54] Russia's Defense Committee announced it will increase spending 60 percent between 2010-13. Procurement priorities are very conventionally based, including land and sea based ICBMs, fighters, submarines and other naval vessels.[55]

We No Longer Fight Industrial Wars

Today's headlines are replete with stories of conflicts involving non-state actors such as Hezbollah, Turkish-Kurds, Chechens, African Pirates, or insurgent groups such as the Boko Haram in Nigeria, exemplifying the prevalence of non-state actors and the preponderance of intrastate conflict. Nevertheless, Smith, mirroring the disjoint between some of the aforementioned national security strategies and actual procurement forecasts, correctly argues that today's western military forces remain wed to the concept of industrial war. He illustrates this paradox while discussing armored warfare.

14

The tank embodies the technology necessary in waging conventional war, as well as the industrial capacity to produce such a weapon. Tanks are expensive, possess ever-increasing technology, and exist in most armies. Nations buy tanks for their mobility, firepower and ability to defeat other tanks. Today, however, they are seldom used in large formations against other armored forces. In fact, Smith convincingly points out that this last occurred in 1991 during Operation Desert Storm; yet in 2011 America possesses 6,242 M1 Main Battle Tanks[56] with a further 8,800 M60 tanks in reserve/storage status.[57]

According to Smith, the Napoleonic wars created the institutional and theoretical foundation for modern industrial warfare. Napoleon mobilized the people using various "levees" to create (and recreate) his Grande Armee, which was organized into mobile and efficient combined arms "corps d'armees" capable of independent action. Clausewitz further improved field armies in post-Napoleonic Prussia through more effective professional training and staff support, creating an effective tool of the state. Fifty years later the American Civil War marked the first truly industrial war when both sides fully mobilized their resources (population, industry, and technology) to support the war. Smith wrote that "[t]he Civil War also established the U.S. way of war; the clear understanding that industrial ability decides a war..."[58]

Russell Wrigley, in his famous book "The American Way of War," argues that America prefers a strategy of annihilation primarily through massing men and techno-logically advanced weapons. Max Boot commented that this viewpoint argues that

> ...the Civil War, WWI, and WWII were won not by tactical or strategic brilliance but by sheer weight of numbers – the awesome destructive power that only a fully mobilized and highly industrialized democracy can bring to bear.[59]

Colin Gray writes that America's wealth created the conditions and predisposition of the US military to conduct military operations on a large scale. According to Gray, once mobilized and equipped, the United States has fought a "rich person's war" unlike poorer countries who are "obliged to wage war frugally" and "fight smarter than rich countries."[60] At the core of America's way of war is the emphasis on firepower over maneuver and being predisposed toward more direct, rather than indirect, strategies.[61] America's "shock and awe" campaign involving precision airstrikes, thousands of long-range rockets and artillery during the 2003 invasion of Iraq epitomizes this mindset. America seeks to apply overwhelming firepower not only to quickly defeat an enemy, but also to reduce casualties to a minimum. America's lavish expenditure of firepower may partially explain the extremely low number of hostile fire casualties in Desert Storm (148) and the initial 2003 invasion of Iraq (84).[62]

America discovered and embraced its industrial superpower status during World War II. The United States mobilized for war and assumed the role as the arsenal of democracy. It produced over 297,000 aircraft, 86,000 tanks, and 8,800 naval vessels.[63] Americans grew accustomed to seeing newsreels of German skies filled with 1,000 bomber raids or Pacific fleets consisting of dozens of carriers and hundreds of aircraft. Americans came to believe and expect that their armed forces would have numerical superiority and the most advanced equipment of any nation on earth. This expectation is just as true today as it was in the 1940's.

By every measure, the United States Department of Defense has embraced this industrial warfare tradition and created a leviathan. America's robust — some would argue exorbitant — defense budgets has enabled US armed forces to be equipped with an absolutely overwhelming number of the highest technological weapons available. The 2010 U.S. defense budget of $693 billion was twice the size of the next six nations (China, France, U.K., Russia, Japan, Germany) plus India combined.[64] In that year, America had 6,242 top-of-the-line M-1 Abrams Main Battle Tanks: two and a half times China's inventory of modern and obsolescent tanks, and four times Russia's similarly mixed inventory.[65] The United States has twice as many fourth-generation aircraft (3,224) as Russia and China combined. In addition, America is the only country in the world to have fifth-generation fighters. It currently has 168 F-22 Raptors — just 21 short of equaling all tactical aircraft in the Royal Air Force. Despite this overwhelming superiority in numbers and technology, America will buy over 2,400 fifth-generation F-35 Joint Strike Fighters (JSF) beginning in 2012.[66] In fact, in a period of shrinking defense budgets, the JSF is the "…largest procurement program in the Department of Defense."[67]

Further, the United States can field 1,404 attack helicopters — the UK has 66. The U.S. Navy boasts 11 battle-ready carriers, whereas the rest of the world combined has four much smaller versions. America's fleet of 538 aerial refueling tankers is larger than the total French Air Force of 328 aircraft.[68] Finally, America has 239 heavy, unmanned aerial vehicles for strategic reconnaissance and strike missions — the rest of the world has 12.[69]

Clearly, America's robust defense budget has provided amply for the country's armed forces, creating significant over-capacity in tanks, strike aircraft, and major naval assets. However, the combined stumbling blocks of America's industrial-war mindset, entrenched political procurement policymaking, and military service branch cultural bias prevent responsive adaptation to the military's new and ever-changing operating environment as espoused in the QDR and Joint Doctrine. For example, Secretary of Defense Robert Gates fought a protracted battle with congressional lawmakers and industrial lobbyists to limit production of the F-22 Raptor to 187 aircraft in order to shift funding to higher priority defense requirements. Gates said in July of 2009, "[i]f we can't bring ourselves to make this tough but straightforward decision — reflecting the judgment of two very different presidents, two different secretaries of defense, two chairmen of the Joint Chiefs of Staff, and the current Air Force secretary and chief of staff — where do we draw the line?"[70] Furthermore, Gates refuted questions of future military threats to America's dominance in air power, emphasizing America's continued technological and numerical overmatch compared to any nation, or combination of nations beyond 2025, despite China's increasing military capabilities. Furthermore, he said, "China will not be able to field a similar plane until about 2025, when the United States will have more than 1,700 F-35s ..."[71]

Smith would argue that Secretary Gates was absolutely on the right track while his opponents' thinking no longer reflects the nature and characteristics of modern war. Unlike the Napoleonic period and the great world wars, "…[war] is no longer a single massive event of military decision that delivers a conclusive political result."[72] Instead, Smith's third major trend indicates that nations enter conflicts seeking a condition for individuals and societies that may take years to accomplish. Examples include promoting democracy, preventing genocide, ensuring rights for ethnic groups, reducing drug trafficking, promoting nation-building and the elimination of terrorists. If Smith's six trends are valid, and interstate wars are and will be virtually non-existent, it is difficult to envision how preparation for an industrial war will easily accomplish these tasks. In today's world, whether or not the military-industrial complex and certain military leaders will admit it, most politicians seek to employ their nations' military forces "...for humanitarian and policing purposes for which they are neither trained nor intended."[73] For instance, America's military is frequently called upon to conduct humanitarian missions. In 2012, the US conducted a "compassionate invasion" of Haiti rendering assistance to a country ravaged by a massive earthquake. America diverted a naval task force, led by an aircraft carrier, and employed almost 10,000 military personnel operating in Haiti or on ships supporting operations.

America's propensity, certainly in the last twenty years, to conduct operations as a multi-national force, illustrating an aversion to risk, are two of Smith's trends in warfare. All major operations have been conducted as part of a multi-national force, including Kosovo (NATO), Desert Storm (25 countries), Iraq (UK, Australia), Afghanistan (NATO), and Libya (NATO, Gulf Cooperation Council). However, multi-national groupings tend to constrain the use of military force in that these armed forces can only conduct those actions sanctioned by the consensus of their members. Also, achieving a meaningful consensus becomes more difficult as the number of members increases. Additionally, even when a consensus is reached, countries will often have national caveats regarding the employment of their forces. Examples include ground units conducting humanitarian missions only or aircraft restricted to air-to-air missions and prohibited from attacking ground targets. Risk aversion also limits the employment of military force as nations seek to prevent casualties in operations – sometimes at the expense of mission accomplishment. Thomas Mahken found American policies designed to protect Soldiers from attack frequently interfered with coalition activities in small wars and peacekeeping operations such as Bosnia and Kosovo. He noted that European officers nicknamed American troops "teenage mutant ninja turtles" because they were required to wear helmets and body armor even in low threat situations."[74]

<u>We Now Fight Wars Among The People</u>

> Smith's third major point is that war will be fought among the people.

> War amongst the people… is different; it is the reality in which the people in the streets and houses and fields – all the people anywhere – are the battlefield. Military engagement can take place anywhere; in the presence of civilians, against civilians, in defense of civilians.[75]

History is replete with instances of wars waged among the people, particularly in recent history. Over 108,000 Iraqi civilians died in the Iraq War/Insurgency between 2003 and 2010. Details of the 4,045 Iraqi civilian casualties in 2010 graphically depict a war among people where coalition and Iraqi state forces caused 113 deaths, while the remaining 3,932 died from anti-occupation forces, bombings, or 'everyday terrorism.' [76] In just four days in March 2012, more than four hundred rockets were fired from from Gaza into southern Israeli urban areas.[77] The insurgent group Boko Haram killed 250 Nigerians in the first two weeks of January 2012 bringing its death toll to 935 since 2009.[78] In just three months an estimated 800,000 Rwandans were killed in 1994 during a governmental campaign of genocide.[79]

Furthermore, terrorism and guerrilla warfare, often cited as "recent developments in warfare," are actually ancient forms of fighting. Terrorism is often incorrectly portrayed as a new occurrence in history linked to Islamic extremists, but this is simply not true; terrorism is neither new nor the exclusive purview of Islamic radicals. In 1946, terrorists exploded a bomb in the King David Hotel in Jerusalem killing 91 people.[80] The terrorists were radical Jews seeking to create the state of Israel by attacking the will of the British Government and by capturing the attention and focus of the media. Other examples of historical terrorism include England's Gunpowder Plot of 1605 attempting to assassinate King James I, American John Brown's raid at Harpers Ferry in 1859, the infamous exploits of the KKK from 1866-present, the Irish Republican Army's bombings in Northern Ireland, and Timothy McVeigh's bombing of the Oklahoma Federal building in 1994.

Examples of guerrilla movements in just the nineteenth century include Britain's battle against the Boers, America's war with Filipino Guerrillas, 1898-1902, and Union and Confederate guerillas during the American Civil War. In Kansas and Missouri, Union aligned "jayhawkers" fought a bitter guerrilla war against Confederate "bushwhackers." In 1862 Arkansas, Confederate guerrillas, attacked military supply lines and units so frequently they turned back a Federal invasion of the state. In 1863, a rebel guerrilla group called Quantrill's Raiders became famous for the Lawrence Kansas Massacre, after killing 182 males and burning 185 buildings.[81]

History also provides abundant examples of proxy wars conducted by third parties (guerrillas, insurgents, tribes) funded by various state and non-state actors. For example, in the French and Indian Wars of the early and mid-1700s, both England and France enlisted Native American allies to serve as their scouts, guides, and shock troops on the North American frontier. During WWI, Britain employed the now legendary T.E. Lawrence to lead the Arab tribes in a guerrilla war against the Turks in the Levant.[82]

Lastly, sustained brutal fighting in population centers is also not a new phenomenon. Constantinople was first sacked by Christians in 1204, then by the Ottomans in 1453. Oliver Cromwell gave no quarter after laying siege to Drogheda, Ireland, in 1649 killing approximately 3,500 people during Britain's civil war.[83] During WWII, major battles in urban areas resulted in hundreds of thousands of civilian casualties including Leningrad (750,000), Manila (100,000), and Berlin (approximately 125,000).[84] Finally, a more recent example is the "...systemic slaughter of at least 2,810 civilians... possibly as many as 5,700..." in Hue City during the Tet offensive of 1968.[85]

What has changed rapidly in the last several decades, however, is the capability of technology employed by today's media to expose people throughout the world rather than in limited locality—to these horrific experiences. The stories and images of human suffering caused by military conflict can be transmitted around the globe instantaneously, becoming a powerful source of political will and impetus for action. It can also have a chilling effect on a military force when reporting significant friendly casualties, civilian deaths, and large scale destruction.

Libya's Civil War of 2011 – A "Smithian" Case Study

The recent civil war in Libya, February-October 2011, is the embodiment of Smith's new reality of war. First, the conflict in Libya was not an interstate war fought between nations employing their full industrial capacity. Instead it was a civil war between forces loyal to Muammar Gaddafi and those supporting the loosely-formed rebel government in Benghazi. The forces doing most of the fighting against the Libyan government were lightly armed Libyan civilians who initially had no centralized military or political leadership; they simply fought Libyan police and military forces to oust

22

Gaddafi. NATO intervened on behalf of the UN "...to protect civilians and civilian populated areas under threat of attack...including Benghazi..."[86]

Second, it was a multinational operation sanctioned by the UN and conducted by NATO forces using extremely risk-averse means. NATO fought a campaign heavily reliant on technology to reduce risk to members of the armed forces and to limit unintended civilian casualties. NATO's tools of war included cruise missiles (112 on the opening day of hostilities alone)[87] delivered from submarines and ships safely offshore, precision bombing from 25,000 feet, missile strikes from unmanned aerial vehicles, and a continued refusal to commit military personnel in a ground combat role (although late in the campaign Britain and France placed a handful of advisors on the ground to assist rebel forces in coordinating air strikes and rebel ground actions).

Third, although difficult to prove conclusively, the media played an important role in garnering worldwide support for the rebels. Months of continuous reporting of the Arab Spring movement involving large scale popular protests against authoritarian governments in Tunisia, Egypt, Bahrain, and Yemen created a largely sympathetic worldwide audience for the Libyan populace. News and social media flooded the world with images of fighting, frequently reporting the destruction and loss of life in small towns and villages. Gaddafi's shocking national speech in which he called the protestors "cockroaches" and urged his followers to go out and attack them in their dens and "cleanse Libya house by House" outraged worldwide opinion.[88] President Obama responded by ordering U.S. military forces into action when fighting moved towards the city of Benghazi and its 700,000 residents. Obama felt compelled to act against Libya because of Gaddafi's "...brutal repression and a looming humanitarian crisis..." and

23

accused Libya's government of civilian massacres and hangings, and the potential of thousands of refugees fleeing to neighboring states.[89] Also, according to Susan Rice, the U.S. Ambassador to the U.N., "the U.S. feared a killing spree in Libya was about to happen earlier this year along the lines of Rwanda's 1994 genocide."[90] America's intervention began with a humanitarian objective that soon transformed into one of regime change.

The war in Libya is just the latest example of the evolution in warfare described by Rupert Smith. America and its allies and partners should take careful note of this campaign when determining national security goals (ends), strategies to meet these goals (ways), and the resources required (means). The United States no longer has the luxury of continuing its cherished preference of procuring the means to fight a "rich man's" war anymore. In an age of constricting national economic power, the alignment of strategies, weapons procurements, and force structures with national goals must be rigorously evaluated. Outdated strategy must be rewritten and reanalyzed and excess or unnecessary force structures and weapons systems ruthlessly reduced or eliminated as necessary to shift resources where needed to accomplish national objectives.

The Way Ahead

> The most serious single threat the US faces to its national security does not come from foreign threats, but from the pressures on defense spending created by these domestic and social and economic trends, and the rising cost of US federal entitlements spending.[91]

The financial constraints imposed on the Department of Defense for several years to come offer an extraordinary opportunity for America to better align its armed forces with the international security paradigm of Rupert Smith. The greatest risk to the Army is creating a maladjusted force structure incapable of performing its roles and functions in the new world of the twenty-first century. Two key considerations are the mix of forces between combat units, particularly heavy/mechanized brigades, sustainment and other enabling units, and the subsequent balance between active and Reserve/National Guard forces. The overarching question that must be asked is what combination of forces is more capable to operate against hybrid threats and intrastate conflicts?

Recent budget cuts forced the US to begin reshaping its armed forces. Several major weapon procurement programs are being eliminated or delayed, and almost 100,000 military personnel will be cut. In the decade ahead, additional budget cuts are almost guaranteed, forcing difficult, and sometimes painful, decisions to be made about force size, composition, and roles. In addition, America should build partner nation capabilities more aggressively to meet local and regional security requirements.

Strategic Procurement Suggestions

America's senior military and political leadership have not yet determined how the armed forces will be cut or reshaped due to known budget cuts. Future cuts are highly likely, further complicating budget planning. But, it is clear that every service has been forced to cut/reduce personnel, equipment, training, and procurement funds. Preliminary announcements seem to indicate several procurement and force structure decisions changes contrary to U.S. strategic policy and military doctrine.

To its credit, America's military leadership is making minor reductions in some areas of over-capacity. The US Army will stop building new tanks or even upgrading current tanks for the next three years. The Navy is cutting or delaying a few vessels. The Air Force cut two small programs: a strategic unmanned reconnaissance program called Global Hawk, and the C-27 twin engine tactical transport aircraft. America is increasing funding for Special Operations to counter terrorism and aligning forces with geographic areas. Aligning units has many benefits. It provides geographic combatant commanders with a ready pool of forces to draw upon for operations. Over time, units will gain significant regional experience. However, despite significant budget reductions America continues to procure expensive weapons systems in areas of overwhelming overmatch such as fighter aircraft and combat helicopters.

America's dominance in fighter aircraft, both technological and numerical, is unquestionable, yet we are procuring over 2,400 F-35 JSF fifth generation fighters in the coming years. The F-35 is an incredibly capable aircraft. It is built with "stealth" capabilities that reduce its radar signature. It can attack ground targets with the most advanced munitions while still retaining the ability to defeat any aircraft in air-to-air combat. It is the "Porsche" of fighter aircraft. However, using the F-35 in many intrastate conflicts would be like driving a Porsche to the grocery store… it could get you there and transport your groceries, but maybe a different car would be cheaper and better suited for such a mundane task.

Why do we need over 2,400 F-35s? Could America's armed forces employ a more economical mix of aircraft and still accomplish national strategic goals? For example, the F-15C, America's premier air-to-air fighter for decades (its air-to-air kill/loss ratio is 95-0), could be upgraded to extend its service life beyond 2030. The cost to upgrade the engines, structure and avionics of the F-15 fleet of approximately 400 aircraft is three billion dollars.[92] Yet America will spend six times that amount buying 19 F-35s in 2012. The cost target is $109-143 million per plane depending on whether it is the Air Force, Marine, or Naval version. In 2011 the annual cost overrun was $771 million or $27.5 million per aircraft.[93] The F-15C is more than a match for any

of the air forces potentially facing America in interstate wars of the near future.

Therefore, is it appropriate for the US to continue exercising the luxury of having a

fighter fleet entirely made of Porsches when national goals can be achieved by carefully

tailoring the right mix of Fords and Volkswagens with a few Porsches?

The US Army also intends to spend billions increasing its over-capacity in

helicopters. America has the largest fleet of transport and attack helicopters in the

world yet it wants to build a thirteenth Combat Aviation Brigade (CAB) in the active

component (AC). The Defense Department FY2012 budget proposal lists "[f]unding the

equipment for a 13th Combat Aviation Brigade" as part of the "Army Modernization

plan."[94] In 2008, Brigadier General Mundt, the director of Army aviation, said "[b]uilding

a new CAB from scratch would cost $3.7 billion and take 3-5 years."[95]

Establishing a 13th CAB received increasing support among senior defense

leadership primarily because of the sustained high deployment rates of aviation units

supporting operations in Iraq and Afghanistan since 2003. The 2011 Army Posture

Statement argued creating a 13th CAB "...[will] relieve the stress on the Aviation force

and provide additional assets for the Operating Force to support Overseas Contingency

Operations."[96] However, the stress on the operational force has already been resolved

through the cessation of operations in Iraq coupled with the rapidly decreasing

operations in Afghanistan, which conclude in 2014. It is hard to justify spending $3.7

creating another CAB when there are 11 AC CABs, and four alone in the National

Guard. Each CAB is designed to support three to five Brigade Combat Teams (BCTs).

Therefore, the current 11 AC CABs can support the Army's future force of 32 AC BCTs.

Furthermore, with no CABs deployed in Iraq or Afghanistan after 2014, its difficult to argue why these 15 CABs are insufficient for future contingency operations.

No discussion about the "right" decisions regarding over-capacity and redundancy would be complete without at least brief evaluation of the Marine Corps, the smallest of America's armed services. This "small" service is bigger in many ways than Germany's Army and Air Force combined. The Marine active component is 22 percent bigger than Germany's equivalent.[97] The Marines have 68 more combat aircraft than the Luftwaffe and 200 more helicopters than the Bundeswehr, Luftwaffe and Deutsche Marine combined. The Marines also have 600 more pieces of artillery (although towed rather than self propelled), five times as many aircraft tankers, and even have the same amount of electronic warfare aircraft as all of Germany's armed forces. But, in a time of shrinking budgets is it not time to examine this over-capacity and make adjustments to either the Marines, Air Force or Army force structure?

Procuring weapons and equipment (the means), is only one facet of national security, but due to political lobbying, domestic employment needs, and the American military tradition of heavy firepower, it receives an inordinate amount of thought and energy among leaders—often at the expense of developing sound long term regional security strategies.

Building Partner Capacity—The Example of Africa

Africa has long been a low priority for the United States as reflected in the paltry amounts of annual US economic and military aid dispensed. However, there are compelling reasons for America to take a more active role developing the economic, military, and human capital capabilities available throughout this continent. Africa is in urgent need of various whole-of-government assistance and increased economic development, and has the greatest number of weak or failed states of any region in the world. Nowhere is the concept of hybrid threats more clearly manifested, or comprehensible, than on the African continent. Clearly, if the United States wishes to practice a more Smithian-type of military strategy on par with recent national security statements, Africa is a place where that is possible.

Africa is unfortunately a poverty stricken, war-torn continent, and will remain so until its nations can consistently provide security and basic services to their citizens. Unfortunately, Africa has more conflicts and crises than any other region in the world. The 2010 Center for Strategic Peace study found Africa had the highest concentration of risk factors (security, governance, economic and social dimensions) to initiate or escalate intra- or interstate wars. African nations accounted for six of the eight extremely fragile states, and sixteen of nineteen high risk states worldwide.[98] This concentration of fragile states fosters conflict and creates regional instability, particularly in the sub-Sahara. The 2009/2010 Human Security Report found "…sub-Saharan Africa accounts for the vast majority of the total number of non-state conflicts that have occurred since 2002. In fact, sub-Saharan Africa accounts for more non-state conflicts than all of the other regions combined."[99]

These intrastate conflicts and crises are mainly fought by combatants equipped with the ubiquitous AK-47, rocket propelled grenades, and Toyota trucks with machine-guns mounted in the back. However, even these low-tech affairs frequently overwhelm the scant resources (economic, military, governmental) of the continents' numerous fragile nation states. Instability and disease often spreads to neighboring states as refugees flee across borders, establishing semi-permanent tent cities numbering tens of thousands of occupants. Violence can also spread as government forces cross borders in pursuit of insurgents or while conducting raids or airstrikes against training camps in safe havens. The lack of national military capabilities and risk to regional stability explains why seven of the U.N.'s fifteen peacekeeping missions are in Africa.[100]

Stability and security throughout Africa continues to become increasingly important to American national interests. Not only does Africa possess huge reserves of natural rare-earth minerals and oil necessary for U.S. defense purposes, but the geo-strategic locations of many African countries offer American strategists both opportunities and risks in ensuring security of the U.S. homeland, American citizens abroad, and international trade. Unfortunately Africa also has the highest potential for perpetual regional instability and conflict. As a result, America is repeatedly found reacting to yet another in a series of crises. Since 1991, US forces have conducted 31 contingency operations in Sub-Saharan Africa alone.[101] These operations varied from humanitarian operations assisting Rwandan refugees who fled to Uganda in 1996, evacuating noncombatants from Liberia in 2003, and on-going counter terrorism activities in the Horn of Africa. Defeating piracy in the Gulf of Aden, Somali Straits, and in the Gulf of Guinea remain American strategic priorities, as does preservation of US-African trade, which increased fourfold since 2000, amounting to $113 billion in 2020. This trade is a critical component of Africa's long term regional and national economic development and supports America's 2010 National Security Strategy for Africa.

In recognition of these facts, America established U.S. African Command (AFRICOM) in 2008, to provide a more focused and integrated combatant command for U.S. interests in Africa. AFRICOM's mission is to strengthen the defense capabilities of

African states and the effectiveness of the AU. These preconceptions are unfortunate because the AU is a highly respected and successful regional organization.

The AU frequently demonstrates a strong political willingness to take actions promoting stability and human rights throughout Africa. Some of its more recent actions include an intervention in Burundi (2003) to impose order, overturning coups in Togo (2005) and Mauritania (2008), and suspending Madagascar (2008) Niger (2010) and Cote d'Ivoire (2010) from the AU for undemocratic behavior. In November the AU declared the Lord's Revolutionary Army a terrorist organization and authorized military operations by a 5,000 man African force to eliminate this group.[102]

The African Union (AU) is strongly committed to conflict prevention and resolution on a regional level using member nation assets. However, the large number of fragile states, systemic economic weakness overall on the continent, and lack of military resources severely hamper the AU's strategic and operational efficacy. The combined (what year?)GNP of the 52 AU member states equals that of the Netherlands. The AU's 2011 budget was only $260 million but its member nations struggled to resource 40 percent of that amount. Furthermore, economic wealth is concentrated in five member nations that provide 75 percent of all AU revenue.[103]

Rapid intervention by military and police forces has proven to be a highly cost-effective solution to Africa's pervasive instabilities when they arise. "After the Rwanda genocide, the United nations released a report which concluded that a small outside force   as few as 5,000 soldiers   could have intervened and stopped the slaughter in its early stages.[104] Several recent conflicts, including those in Sierra Leone and Liberia, demonstrate that early intervention (7-14 days after conflict initiation) by a brigade-sized

31

force could have defeated or prevented conflict escalation. Therefore, building the AU's rapid deployment capability could improve stability and security in Africa. Regional and national economic development, if conducted correctly, can also alleviate or even remove many of the social and economic conditions that often result in conflicts. However, while economic development can potentially eliminate economic and social causes of African conflict, fragile and corrupt governments often frustrate these efforts, as America has rediscovered after spending hundreds of billions of dollars in Iraq and Afghanistan. Unfortunately, the risk of conflict in Africa is immediate and requires a swift resolution thus facilitating longer-term economic developments to mature.

In 2003, the AU established an African Standby Force (ASF) of five standby brigades, with one multi-national brigade from each of Africa's five regions. These forces are intended to deploy in advance of the UN as they recently did with the African Union Mission in Sudan in the Darfur and the AU mission in Somalia. The primary motivation for a rapid response by African military forces (with organic civil, political, and police elements) "was largely 'never to allow another genocide like Rwanda'..." with its widespread genocide and crimes against humanity. [105] However willing the AU is to create and employ the ASF, the command and control capabilities of which continue to improve, it is heavily reliant on non-African financial support to train and equip these regional brigades.

Focus on the Sub-Region of West Africa

There are many programs providing training, aid, and assistance to Africa from various countries and international organizations. Perhaps it would be more beneficial to focus resources on one sub-regional force at a time rather than risk spreading resources so thin that they fail to adequately train any of the forces. Several nations provide bilateral aid and training for African Union forces. France and the UK have colonial ties with West Africa, have built training centers in Mali, Nigeria and Ghana, and fund portions of mission training required before peacekeeping units deploy for operations. The challenge is coordinating and matching various non-African funding and training goals with those of the AU. The US should begin to strengthen military- to-military training, increase individual Soldier skills, and increase Department of State aid promoting democracy in West Africa.

Several reasons present themselves regarding why the US should begin prioritizing its efforts to build the capability of the East Africa stand-by force (Economic Community of West African States [ECOWAS] stand-by force or ESF) First, concentrating on one African region at a time best focuses resources and builds capability more rapidly. Efforts should begin with the best regional force and work down to the worst. The ESF is experienced and serves as the "go-to" force for the AU. Improving the ESF's logistical capabilities and individual soldier training would rapidly improve the capabilities of the most likely force the AU would employ in conflict prevention or resolution.

Second, of the AU's five regions, the Western region has the highest level of political willingness to engage in peacekeeping operations. Member nations such as Ghana, Senegal, and Nigeria are firmly committed to UN and AU peacekeeping missions, and consistently provide large numbers of peacekeepers. The Western region's serious commitment to peacekeeping is a reflection of Nigeria's regional leadership. Nigeria sets the example by having military or police personnel deployed in every UN and AU peacekeeping mission. The South regional force is the next best force but the East, North and Central regions are beset by so many crises that our strategic means would be wasted supporting difficult ways toward almost unattainable ends, at least for the short-term.

Third, the stability of West Africa is more important to U.S. interests economically and politically by defeating Al Qaeda-linked terrorist groups in Nigeria and Mali. Nigeria is America's largest trading partner, more than twice as much as the next country, South Africa. Also, importation of Nigerian oil continues to increase while Ghana is just beginning to exploit its offshore oilfields. These oil revenues are vital to the economic growth and stability of West Africa. Home-grown Nigerian terrorist organizations such as Boko Horam seek to cooperate with Al Qaeda, encouraging violent extremism and the creation of an Islamic state. This would clearly imperil American interests.

The best strategy to increase the capability of the ESF is focusing on training Soldiers rather than giving or selling large amounts of high-tech equipment. Training should focus on the critical skills required to perform peacekeeping missions as part of a UN or AU force. Peacekeeping forces should be light, infantry-centric, sufficiently armed to defeat lightly armed forces but have the ability to call upon and deploy heavy armor, artillery, and vehicles when required. After all, the national armed forces of many African nations are equipped with some heavy equipment, albeit obsolescent and in small numbers. Unfortunately, some first-world countries want to sell advanced weapons systems to generate money and make African nations into a mirror image of the exporting countries' armed forces. This is extremely dangerous policy, both to African regional stability and to African economic growth, as a nation's armed forces must be economically sustainable over the long term. Significantly increasing manpower or buying large numbers of high-tech weapons can become economically burdensome for poorer nations. This burden may force governments to take funds from the economic developmental programs that ultimately would have created long-term social and political stability and spend it to maintain their armed forces. The United States should discourage nations from creating unaffordable armed forces that require foreign aid to maintain.

The U.S. should also expand the size and scope of its engagements with Africa through the National Guard Partnership Program. Several years ago this program assigned four states to conduct regular training with West African countries (North Dakota-Ghana, Michigan-Liberia, California-Nigeria, Vermont-Senegal). This program builds basic Soldier skills such as marksmanship, patrolling, non-lethal crowd control techniques, and military job skills. The program has the advantage of establishing long term relationships of military units and governments.

As an example, the Tennessee Air National Guard spent over a year building the maintenance skills of Nigerian air force personnel while rebuilding a C-130 cargo aircraft. The Tennessee airmen taught maintenance skills such as preventive maintenance procedures, acceptance test flight checks, and records maintenance. These maintenance skills are critically important to AU operations. AU forces generally lack the ability to logistically sustain themselves, quickly project power by moving personnel and equipment, or provide humanitarian relief to remote areas. Therefore, maintaining the readiness of Nigeria's fleet of eight C-130's is vitally important to mission success.[106]

Much of America's military excellence is due to a superb professional corps of non-commissioned officers (NCOs). In addition to NCO professional development course exchange programs, the Department of State (DoS) offers leadership courses to African Soldiers and civilians through International Military Education Training (IMET). In 2009, the DoS spent $19 million for approximately 900 military and civilians from 44 African countries to receive education and training in the U.S. or through local courses conducted by U.S. cadre.[107] IMET program objectives include increasing relations between representatives of various nations and educating personnel to instill and maintain democratic values. America would do well to continue and expand the program.

Protecting American citizens by building the anti-piracy capabilities of African states is another vital national interest. Piracy off the horn of Africa and in the Gulf of Guinea has killed Americans and interfered with international trade. The United States and other countries have donated surplus naval vessels, conducted maritime security training with African naval units, and participated in multi-national security operations. As a result, African naval forces are increasingly capable of combating piracy and enforcing rule of law. America donated a surplus 368 foot high Endurance Coast Guard Cutter to Nigeria in 2011 which significantly increased the ability of Nigeria to long range sustained maritime patrols. Another benefit was that by donating this vessel America will saved "…approximately $10 million in disposal costs for [the] cutter."[108]

These approaches to training are extremely cost-beneficial when compared to using U.S. forces to maintain security. Susan Rice, the US Ambassador to the UN, said "[i]f the US was to act on its own – unilaterally – and deploy its own forces in many of these countries, for every dollar that the US would spend, the UN can accomplish the Mission for twelve cents."[109] Significantly improved military capabilities can be achieved by focusing resources for the right purposes and then shifting resources to build capacity in another nation. In the budgetarily constrained future environment, increasing the AU's military capabilities will more than pay back the costs of training and equipping AU peacekeeping forces. Early intervention by well-trained AU forces can ensure that the U.S. and other non-African nations will not always have to provide direct military and monetary support when crises occur.

The Significance of Nigeria

The U.S. should further focus its development and training resources into a few countries within sub-regions. Comparing the desired end state with existing capabilities will allow for identification of specific deficiencies, their early correction, and proper resourcing requirements.

Nigeria plays an important role supporting the AU in peacekeeping operations and in the West African force (ESF). Nigeria is the most populous African country, has re-embraced democracy, and is blessed with a vibrant economy. Nigeria is a very dynamic and influential regional leader and is largely responsible for the ESF being such a capable multi-national force, as evidenced by two largely successful operations in Sierra Leone and Liberia. Nigeria is also the primary force provider for ESF and the biggest contributor for UN/AU peacekeeping missions. Further, Nigeria is the world's fourth largest contributor of UN peacekeepers (5,667), spending "about $10 billion on peace-keeping ventures in Liberia and Sierra Leone and [losing] 1,000 in the process."[110] Economically, Nigeria is a growing hegemonic power with a GNP growth rate of 21 percent over the past three years. U.S. Nigerian trading totaled $34.5 billion;

37

ten times the amount of 2000. In testimony before the Senate, Johnnie Carson, the Assistant Secretary, Bureau of African Affairs, testified "…Nigeria is simply too important to Africa and too important to the United States and the international community for us not to be concerned and engaged. Widespread instability in Nigeria could have a tsunami-like ripple effect across West Africa and the global community"[111]

The success of democracy in Nigeria is the key to its future political stability, economic progress and leadership ability. Nigeria became a regional force for good when it returned to democracy in May,1999. Since that time living standards have improved and the government is responding to domestic violence and terrorism in a lawful and responsible manner. The Department of State must continue providing ample aid to Nigeria to strengthen democratic institutions and governance, while the Department of Defense. should increase training exercises, military exchanges, and U.S. National Guard partnerships programs to expand the competency of the Nigerian armed forces. All of this will also positively affect Nigeria's participation in the standing anti-piracy maritime security task force. America should additionally identify critical Nigerian capability gaps and seek to find surplus equipment that can be given or sold to the West African nation.

Conclusion

Despite some shortcomings, General Smith's thesis convincingly challenges several core tenets of current strategic thought regarding the demise of interstate war and the industrial war mindset of the U.S. Many western nations are at a pivotal point in time where budget constraints are forcing leaders to cut and reshape their forces. Today's decisions will impact the ability of national armed forces to successfully achieve their national strategic policy objectives.

The preponderance of research confirms Smith's thesis that intrastate war is the predominant form of conflict, both currently and in the future. National strategies agree that hybrid threats – with terrorism, Weapons of Mass Destruction/Proliferation, and cyber attacks are the greatest challenges to the security environment today. Despite this shared vision, nations have adopted widely divergent ways and means to meet these threats. Germany is reshaping its army by reducing the number of Soldiers and creating a tiered Army, consisting of 1/3 high intensity units, and 2/3 stabilization forces. Of all the national policies discussed in this paper, Germany's strategy and force structure best mirrors its strategic policy. The UK's actions to reduce its overall military, cutting armored forces, and increase funding for Special Forces follow its national policy. However, the UK is still committed to expensive high-tech weaponry including the Euro Typhoon Fighter, the F-35 JSF and its two Queen Elizabeth-class aircraft carriers. China and Russia's procurement plans and questionable funding make it nearly impossible to speak with confidence on what they will actually procure and what military capabilities they will likely have. However, Russia continues to exhibit paranoia regarding NATO and is apparently investing heavily in conventional forces. Australia stresses the threats of terrorism and cyber attacks but has committed to obtaining high-tech weapons systems with seemingly little direct application to counter terrorism or defending against hybrid threats.

America should take three actions. First, military leaders should critically examine their procurement strategies and ensure the means available correspond to national security policy. Current and anticipated future budget cuts present an extraordinary opportunity for each of the services to question what capabilities must remain in their service, be shifted to another, or possibly be reduced or eliminated. The Chiefs of Staff must scrutinize areas of redundancy and overmatch beginning with the JSF, Army helicopters, and Marine Corps capabilities. America can no longer afford the luxury of wasteful redundancies and unnecessary force structure.

Second, America should continue to strengthen international and regional security organizations, particularly in Africa. As Smith wrote, due to the paradigm shift underway nations seeks to take action as part of a multinational force authorized by an international body. Africa remains the most likely region to experience intrastate conflict and regional instability. The UN has found that the ability to send a force of approximately 5,000 personnel within 7-14 days of a conflict's commencement can significantly reduce or prevent casualties and possibly stop the conflict. Ensuring such a force is trained and prepared for deployment is a more fiscally prudent and effective solution than deploying US Soldiers, Airmen, or Marines after the local situation on the ground has gone critical.

Third, America should select key partners in Africa and develop appropriate strategies that build their capabilities and contribute to an increased regional capacity to resolve conflicts and instability quickly. Nigeria in particular offers an excellent option in this regard as it is one of Africa's major powers and currently leads the continent in conflict prevention/resolution.

Acceptance of General Smith's paradigm that interstate industrial wars are now obsolescent will necessitate an enormous transformation in American military strategy and supporting procurement policies. This transformation, perhaps already underway in some respects, is woefully incomplete but will ultimately create a military force better-suited to successfully operate in the new paradigm of Smithian warfare. Africa, a continent at once replete both with strategic promise and strategic threats, will be a likely stage upon which this new paradigm will be played out. The United States and its allies cannot afford to allow the African nations to slide into intrastate chaos and instability and must immediately begin to implement a successful continent-wide strategy focusing on strengthening the AU by increasing the capabilities of its regional stand-by forces. Failure to implement this strategy will result in an ominous realization of the worst of Rupert Smith's theoretical predictions, not only for Africa, but perhaps for the world as a whole.

Endnotes

[1] General Rupert Smith, *The Utility of Force: The Art of War in the Modern World* (New York: Vintage Books, 2008),

[2] Ibid., 3.

[3] Ibid., 271.

[4] Ibid., xiv.

[5] "In the 1950s there were on average between six and seven international conflicts being fought around the world each year; in the new millennium the average has been less than one." Human Security Report Project, *Human Security Report 2009/2010: The Causes of Peace and The Shrinking Costs of War,* (New York: Oxford University Press, 2011), 21. http://www.hsrgroup.org/human-security-reports/20092010/text.aspx (accessed January 3, 2012).

[6] Smith, *The Utility of Force, 19-20.*

[7] Mary Kaldor, "Elaborating the 'New War' Thesis," in Isabelle Duyvesteyn and Jan Angstrom, eds., *Rethinking the Nature of War* (New York: Frank Cass, 2005), 221. quoted in Bart Shuurman, "Clausewitz and the New Wars Scholars," *Parameters* 40, no1 (Spring 2010): 89-100, in ProQuest (accessed September 13, 2011).

[8] Martin van Creveld, *On Future War* (London: Brassey's, 1991), ix. quoted in Bart Shuurman, "Clausewitz and the New Wars Scholars," *Parameters* 40 no.1 (Spring 2010): 89-100, in ProQuest (accessed September 13, 2011).

[9] Newman referenced a 2003 study by the University of Maryland that the "…incidence of interstate war has shown a slight increase since 1997." Armed Conflict and Intervention Project, 2003. 'Global Conflict Trends', Center for System Peace, University of Maryland; available at http://members.aol.com/CSPmgm/cspframe.htm (December 2003). Edward Newman, "The 'New Wars' Debate: A Historical Perspective is Needed," *Security Dialogue* 35 no.2 (June 2004): 173, International Peace Research Institute, Oslo, http://sdi.sagepub.com/content/ 35/2/173 (accessed September 15, 2011).

[10] Kalevi J. Holsti, *The State, War, and the State of War* (Cambridge: Cambridge University Press, 1996), 24.

[11] The author did not find a study disputing that intrastate conflict /wars is the predominant form of warfare since 1946 (the beginning reference point for many studies). The following studies by individuals or research institutes found intrastate conflicts as the dominant form of worldwide conflict:

"…77 percent of 164 wars were internal…" Ibid., 21.

"Societal warfare has been the predominant mode of warfare since the mid-1950's…" Monty G. Marshall and Benjamin R. Cole, *Global Report 2011: Conflict Governance, and State Fragility* (Vienna, Virginia, USA: Center for Systemic Peace, December 1, 2011), 4, http://www.systemicpeace.org/GlobalReport2011.pdf (accessed November 5, 2011).

"For the seventh year running, no major interstate conflict was active in 2010. Over the decade 2001-2010, only 2 out of the total of 29 major armed conflicts have been interstate." Stockholm International Peace Research Institute, *SIPRI Yearbook 2011: Armaments, Disarmament, International Security*, 4, http://www.sipri.org/yearbook/2011/02/02A

The Correlates of War 1816-2007 database v4.0 lists only two interstate conflicts (Afghanistan and Iraq) and 23 intrastate wars since 2001 http://www.correlatesofwar.org/

The Heidelberg Institute for International Conflict Resolution found nearly three quarters of the 365 conflicts studied were intrastate. Heidelberg Institute for International Conflict Research, "2009 Conflict Barometer," 2, http://hiik.de/en/konfliktbarometer/pdf/ConflictBarometer_2009.pdf (accessed February 10, 2012).

"The overwhelming majority of armed conflicts are now fought *within* states. These intrastate conflicts have relatively low annual battle-death tolls on average and have made up an increasing proportion of all conflicts since the end of World War II. In the late 1940s, they made up little over half of all conflicts; by the early 1990s, their share was closer to 90 percent." Human Security Report Project, *Human Security Report 2009/2010,* (Oxford University Press, New York, 2011), 160, http://www.hsrgroup.org/docs/Publications/HSR20092010/ 20092010HumanSecurityReport-Part3-TrendsInHumanInsecurity.pdf

Since 1946, intrastate conflicts are more frequent than interstate. From 1946 to the mid-1970s intrastate wars outnumbered interstate wars by at least two-to-one. Since the mid-1970s the annual number of intrastate/interstate conflicts was 20-38 and 0-4 respectively. J. Joseph Hewitt, Jonathan Wilkenfeld, and Ted Robert Gurr, "Peace and Conflict 2012 Executive Summary," Center for International Development and Conflict Management, University of

Maryland, p18, http;//www.cidcm.umd.edu/pc/executive_summary/exec_sum_2012.pdf (accessed December 30, 2011).

[12] For example, Holsti excluded wars of "national liberation" and included armed interventions involving significant loss of life. Holsti, *The State, War, and the State of War*, Table 2, 24. Also, "The issue of whether to include wars of colonial liberation as "international" conflicts is contested. Some scholars count them as civil wars within a colonial power. Others, including [the Uppsala Conflict Data Program datasets], believe they are sui generis and should be treated as separate from both interstate and intrastate conflicts. UDCP uses the term "extrastate"..." Human Security Report Project, Human Security Report 2009-2010, 22. http://www.hsrgroup.org/human-security-reports/20092010/text.aspx (accessed December 6, 2011).

[13] Ibid., 159-161.

[14] Monty G. Marshall, "Warlist: Major Episodes of Political Violence 1946-2008," linked from Center for Systemic Peace Home Page, http://www.systemicpeace.org/warlist.htm (accessed December 30, 2011).

[15] Heidelberg Institute for International Conflict Research, *2009 Conflict Barometer*, 84.

[16] Heidelberg Institute for International Conflict Research, Methodological Approach, http://hiik.de/en/methodik/index.html (accessed January 3, 2012).

[17] Heidelberg Institute for International Conflict Research Website, Methodology Page: Methodology Since 2003, http://hiik.de/en/methodik/methodik_ab_2003.html, (accessed December 30, 2011).

[18] Heidelberg Institute for International Conflict Research, University of Heidelberg, 21. http://hiik.de/en/konfliktbarometer/pdf/ConflictBarometer_2008.pdf (accessed December 30, 2011).

[19] Monty G. Marshall, "Major Episodes of Political Violence 1946-2011," Center for Systemic Peace, http://www.systemicpeace.org/warlist.htm (accessed January 3, 2012).

[20] After 2002, South Ossetians could apply for a Russian passport without even leaving their homes. "Reportedly...up to 90 percent of South Ossethia's population of under 100,000 used this opportunity to acquire Russian citizenship." SZ RF 2002, No. 22, Item 2031 quoted in Law Library Of Congress, Russian Federation Legal Aspects of War in Georgia, 11, http://www.loc.gov/law/help/russian-georgia-war.pdf (accessed December 30,2011).

Below is the article which led to the Law Library of Congress Article

Kristopher Natoli, Weaponizing Nationality: An Analysis of Russia's Passport Policy in Georgia, Boston University International Law Hournal VOL 28:389, 391-2, http://www.bu.edu/law/central/jd/organizations/journals/international/documents/Natoli_WeaponizingNationality.pdf (accessed December 30 2011).

[21] Roger N. McDermott, "Russia's Conventional Armed Forces and the Georgian War," Parameters 39.1 (Spring 2009): 65-80, in ProQuest (accessed August 23, 2011).

[22] Nineteen decolonizing wars of "national liberation" were not included in the 164 wars noted. Holsti, *The State, War, and the State of War,* 21.

[23] Ted Robert Gurr, Monty G. Marshall, Deepa Khosla, "Peace and conflict 2001; A Global Survey of Armed Conflicts, Self-Determination Movements, and Democracy, 2001, Center for International Development and Conflict Management (CIDCM) University of Maryland, Http://www.bsos.umd.edu/cidcm (accessed September 15, 2011).

[24] Heidelberg Institute for International Conflict, "*2009 Conflict Barometer,*" 2, http://hiik.de/en/konfliktbarometer/pdf/ConflictBarometer_2009.pdf (accessed February 10, 2012).

[25] Ibid., 2.

[26] Hewitt, Wilkenfeld, Gurr, "Peace and Conflict 2012 Executive Summary," 18.

[27] Ibid., 19.

[28] Ibid., Figure 4.1, 19.

[29] Monty G. Marshall and Jack Gladstone, "Global Report on Conflict, Governance and State Fragility 2007: Gauging System Performance and Fragility in the Globalization Era," *Foreign Policy Bulletin,* Vol 17, No.1, (Winter 2007), Cambridge University Press, New York, 2007, 7.

[30] Nobelprize.org, "Wars in the 20th Century and Nobel Peace Prize Statistics", http://www.nobelprize.org/educational/peace/conflictmap/readmore.html (accessed September 22, 2011).

[31] Department of Defense, Quadrennial Defense Review Report, February 1, 2010, Department of Defense, 42. http://www.defense.gov/ qdr/qdr%20as%20of%2029jan10%201600.PDF (accessed 24 Nov 2011).

[32] U.S. Joint Chiefs of Staff, *Doctrine for the Armed Forces of the United States,* Joint Publication 1, Change 1, (Washington C.C.: U.S. Joints Chiefs of Staff, March 29, 2009), x. http://www.dtic.mil/doctrine/new_pubs/jp1.pdf (accessed December 1, 2011).

[33] Ibid, 9.

[34] U.S. Department of the Army, *Unified Land Operations,* ADP 3-0, (Washington D.C: Department of the Army, October 2011) 4. http://usacac.army.mil/cac2/Doctrine2015/index.asp (accessed March 14, 2012).

[35] GEN Martin E. Dempsey, *Statement of Chairman of the Joint Chiefs of Staff before the Senate Armed Forces Committee, FY13 Department of Defense Budget*, February 14, 2012, 3, http://armed-services.senate.gov/statemnt/2012/02%20February/Dempsey%2002-14-12.pdf (accessed March 11, 2012).

[36] David Cameron, *A Strong Britain in an Age of Uncertainty: The National Security Strategy* (Norwich, U.K.: Stationary Officer, OCT 2010), forward, http://www.direct.gov.uk/

prod_consum_dg/groups/dg_digitalassets/@dg/@en/documents/digitalasset/dg_191639.pdf (accessed November 24, 2011).

[37] Ibid., 14.

[38] Ibid., 34.

[39] James Kirkup, "Navy aircraft carrier will be sold after three years – and never carry jets," *The Telegraph*, November 27, 2011, http://www.telegraph.co.uk/news/uknews/defence/8072041/Navy-aricraft-carrier-will-be-sold-after-three-years-and-never-carry-jets.html (accessed November 26,2011).

[40] Ibid.

[41] Australian Department of Defence, *Defending Australia in the Asia Pacific Century: Force 2030: Defence White Paper, 2009*, 49. http://www.defence.gov.au/publications/White%20Paper%20Booklet.pdf *(*accessed November 24, 2011).

[42] Ibid., 22.

[43] Ibid., 58.

[44] Ibid., 70-72.

[45] South African Government Information, *White Paper on National Defence for the Republic of South Africa: Defence in a Democracy, May 1996*, chapter 4, paragraph 5.1. www.info.gov.za/whitepapers/1996/defencwp.htm (accessed November 26, 2011).

[46] Anton Kruger, Institute for Security Studies (Tshwane/Pretoria), "South Africa: Defence v Finance, the Long-term Implications for Local Security," November 2, 2010, http://allafrica.com/stories/201011020797.html, (accessed December 18, 2011).

[47] Federal Republic of Germany Ministry of Defence, Defense Policy Guidelines, May 27, 2011, Section II The Strategic Security Environment, http://www.google.com/url?sa=t&rct=j&q=&esrc=s&frm=1&source=web&cd=1&ved=0CCEQFjAA&url=http%3A%2F%2Fwww.bmvg.de%2Fresource%2Fresource%2FMzEzNTM4MmUzMzMyMmUzMTM1MzMyZTM2MzIzMDMwMzAzMDMwMzAzMDY3NmY2ODMyNjEzMTc2NjgyMDIwMjAyMDIw%2F110527%2520VPR%2520engl.pdf&ei=-AAzT77NLoLb0QGSzrHUBw&usg=AFQjCNFLMcRpGyzIvZ1XPeoQsEemYujVlw&sig2=xDb30LwW0cLg_ghFCDqM3w (accessed February 7,2011).

[48] Federal Ministry of Defense, *White Paper 2006 on German Security Policy and the Future of the Bundeswehr*, (Federal Ministry of Defence: Berlin) 17-18, http://merln.ndu.edu/whitepapers/ germany_white_paper_2006.pdf (accessed January 1, 2012).

[49] Ibid, 9.

[50] Total Bundeswehr force structure personnel percentages by category are: Response Forces(14%), Stablisation Forces (28%) and Support Forces which include logistics, medical

and intelligence support and training cadre (58%). Total personnel strength listed in the 2006 White Paper was 252,500. Ibid., 80.

51 The White Paper wrote that"…terrorist, separatist and extremist activities run amok." Separatists include Taiwan, Tibet and East Turkistan independence groups. Information Office of the State Council of the People's Republic of China, China's national Defense in 2010, Downloaded from the official Chinese Government English Translation at http://china.or.cn/government/whitepaper/node_7114675.htm on March 31, 2011 and accessed on http://merln.ndu.edu/whitepapers/China_English2010.pdf, 4, (accessed December 10, 2011).

52 Ibid., 29.

53 The Russian Federation consists of 46 provinces, 21 republics and 15 other entities (Krays and the Federal Cities of Moscow and St. Petersburg). Dr. Marko Beljac, Military Doctrine of Russia, February 5, 2010, Russia's New Military Doctrine in English, Nuclear Resonances, paragraphs 8 and 9, http://scisec.net/?p=231 (accessed December 8, 2011).

54 Reuters, "Russia says a fifth of defense budget stolen," *Tehran Times*, August 11,2011, http://old.tehrantimes.com/index_View.asp?code=241361 (accessed February 7, 2012).

55 Forecast International, "Russia Releases Details on Defense Spending through 2013," October 14, 2010, Defence Talk.com Global Defense & Military Portal, http://www.defensetalk.com/russia-releases-details-on-defense-spending-through2013-29437/ (accessed December 8, 2011).

56 Authors note: although the America and Iraq both fielded large numbers of tanks, tank vs. tank engagements, particularly involving company sized engagements, were relatively scarce in 2003. Many Iraqi regular units abandoned their vehicles without a fight while irregular fedayeen forces conducted a stubborn defense throughout Iraq. Reference for number of tanks: The International Institute for Strategic Studies, *The Military Balance 2011*, (London: Arundel Press, March 2011), 34, 58.

57 Military Periscope.com, Nations/Alliances/Geographic Regions: USA, http://www.militaryperiscope.com/nations/usa/usa/army/index.html#equip (accessed September 9, 2011).

58 Smith, *The Utility of Force,* 90.

59 Max Boot, "The New American Way of War," *Foreign Affairs*, July/August 2003, 82, no.4, 41.

60 Colin S Gray, "The American Way of War: Critique and Implications," *Rethinking the Principles of War*," Anthony D. McIvor, (Annapolis, Maryland: Naval Institute Press, 2005), 30.

61 Thomas G. Mahnken, "The American Way of War in the Twenty-first Century", *Democracies and Small Wars*, (Frank Cass, London, 2003). 74-75.

62 Boot, "New American Way of War," 43.

63 Mahnken, "American Way of War in the Twenty-first Century," 77.

[64] The International Institute for Strategic Studies, *The Military Balance 2011*, 34, 111, 245.

[65] Ibid., 34.

[66] Congressional Research Service, F-35 Joint Strike Fighter (JSF) Program, February 28, 2012, http://fulltextreports.com/2012/02/28/crs-f-35-joint-strike-fighter-jsf-program/ (accessed March 11, 2012).

[67] Jeremiah Gertler, *F-35 Joint Strike Fighter (JSF) Program RL30563*, Congressional Research Service, February 16, 2012, 1, http://www.fas.org/sgp/crs/weapons/RL30563.pdf (accessed March 14, 2012).

[68] The International Institute for Strategic Studies, *The Military Balance 2011*, 34, 107.

[69] Ibid., 34.

[70] Greg Jaffe, "Gates Makes Impassioned Case for Ending F-22 Program," Washington Post, July 17, 2009, http://www.washingtonpost.com/wp-dyn/content/article/2009/07/16/AR2009071603872.html (accessed October 13, 2011).

[71] Ibid.

[72] Smith, *The Utility of Force,* 20.

[73] Ibid., 12.

[74] Mahnken, "The American Way of War in the Twenty-first Century," 76.

[75] Smith, *The Utility of Force,* 6.

[76] Iraq Body Count, http://www.iraqbodycount.org/analysis/numbers/2010/ (accessed February 7, 2012).

[77] Anav Silverman, "Israel's South Surviving Next Round of Gaza Rocket Fire," *Huffington Post,* March 13, 2012 (accessed march 20,2012).

[78] Reuters in Abuja, The Guardian, UK, "Nigerian death toll from Boko Haram attacks 'nears 1,000,' January 24, 2012, http://www.guardian.co.uk/world/2012/jan/24/boko-haram-killed-nearly-1000 (accessed February 7, 2012).

[79] BBC News, "Rwanda: How the genocide happened," http://news.bbc.co.uk/2/hi/1288230.stm (accessed February 7, 2012).

[80] Seattle Times, "Two Peoples, One Land; Understanding the Israeli-Palestinian Conflict," May 12, 2002, http://seattletimes.nwsource.com/news/nation-world/mideast/revolts/ (accessed September 18, 2011).

[81] History.com, This Day in History, August 21,1863 Guerillas massacre residents of Lawrence, Kansas, http://www.history.com/this-day-in-history/sack-of-lawrence-kansas (accessed February 7, 2012).

[82] Lowell Thomas' multimedia show in 1919-1924 was seen by more than 4 million people between 1919-1924. The 1962 movie Lawrence of Arabia further expanded worldwide awareness of this historic figure. http://www.cliohistory.org/thomas-lawrence/lawrence/ (accessed January 2, 2012). T.E. Lawrence's "Seven Pillars of Wisdom: A Triumph is on the counterinsurgency training command – Afghanistan recommended reading list, http://www.cusnc.navy.mil/ctf-ia/documents/COIN%20Recommended%20Reading%20List.pdf (accessed January 2, 2012).

[83] Barry, Taylor, "Siege and slaughter at Drogheda," *Military History*, October 1999, ProQuest http://search.proquest.com/docview/212660961 (accessed February 10,2012).

[84] The siege of Leningrad lasted over 900 days and resulted in over 750,000 civilian deaths. ABC News. http://www.abc.net.au/radionational/programs/latenightlive/the-siege-of-leningrad/3665600 (accessed February 10,2012). Over 100,00 civilians died in battle for Manila during February 3 – March 3, 1945. http://www.ww2museums.com/article/7744/Memorial-Civilian-Casualties-Manila.htm (accessed February 10,2012).

[85] James, Clifford, "Forgotten Massacre at Hue," Vietnam, 14. 5 (February 2002), ProQuest http://search.proquest.com/docview/195760985 (accessed February 10,2010).

[86] UN Security Council SC/10200, March 17,2011, "Security Council Approves 'No-Fly Zone' over Libya, authorizing 'all necessary measures' to protect civilians, by vote of 10 in favor with 5 abstentions," paragraph 4. http://www.un.org/News/Press/docs/2011/sc10200.doc.htm (accessed March 14,2012).

[87] Associated Press, "Libya hit with 112 cruise missiles in first phase of allied assault," *Sun Times*, March 19, 2011, http://www.suntimes.com/news/world/4405622-418/story.html (accessed September 18, 2011).

[88] BBC News, "Libya protests: Defiant Gadaffi refuses to quit." February 22, 2011, http://www.bbc.co.uk/news/world-middle-east-12544624 (accessed March 14,2012).

[89] White House Office of the Press Secretary, "Remarks by the President in Address to the nation on Libya," National Defense University, Washington, D.C., March 28, 2011 http://www.whitehouse.gov/the-press-office/2011/03/28/remarks-president-address-nation-libya (accessed February 12, 2012).

[90] AP, "U.S. feared Libyan killing spree, Rice tells Rwanda," CBS News, http://www.cbsnews.com/8301-501710_162-57330393/us-feared-libyan-killing-spree-rice-tells-rwanda/ (accessed February 12, 2012).

[91] Anthony H. Cordesman, *"The New US Defense Strategy and the Priorities and Changes in FY2013 Budget,"* Center for Strategic and International Studies, January 30, 2012, 3, http://csis.org/files/publication/120128_US_New_Strategy_FY13_Budget.pdf (accessed February 17, 2012).

[92] Federation of American Scientists, "F-15 Eagle", March 14, 2012, http://www.fas.org/programs/ssp/man/uswpns/air/fighter/f15.html (accessed March 14, 2012).

[93] Amy Butler, "F-35 LRIP 4 Jets 7% Over Target Cost," *Aviation Week*, December 02, 2011 http://www.aviationweek.com/aw/generic/story_channel.jsp?channel=defense&id=news/asd/2011/12/02/01.xml

[94] Office of the Under Secretary of Defense (Comptroller)/CFO, *United States Department of Defense Fiscal Year 2012 Budget Request Overview*, February 2011, 4-7 http://comptroller.defense.gov/defbudget/fy2012/FY2012_Budget_Request_Overview_Book.pdf (accessed February 18, 2012).

[95] Rotor&Wing, "U.S. Army Wants to Form 12th Combat Aviation Brigade," May 1, 2008, http://www.aviationtoday.com/rw/military/attack/21519.html (accessed February 17, 2012).

[96] Department of the Army, 2011 *Army Posture Statement*, July 2011, https://secureweb2.hqda.pentagon.mil/VDAS ArmyPostureStatement/2011/information papers/ PostedDocument.asp?id=325 (accessed February 19, 2012).

[97] The International Institute for Strategic Studies, *The Military Balance 2010*, (Routledge, London, 2010), 36-37 & 134-136.

[98] Monty G. Marshall and Benjamin R. Cole, State Fragility Index and Matrix 2010, Center for Systemic Peace, http://www.systemicpeace.org/SFImatrix2010c.pdf (accessed March 14, 2012).

[99] Human Security Report Project, Human Security Rpt 2009-2010, 174. http://www.hsrgroup.org/human-security-reports/20092010/text.aspx (accessed December 6, 2011).

[100] United Nations Peacekeeping Operations, FACT Sheet: 31 December, 2011, http://www.un.org/en/peacekeeping/documents/bnote010101.pdf (accessed January 25, 2011).

[101] Mike Denning, "A Prayer for Marie: Creating an Effective African Standby Force," *Parameters*, Winter 2004/2005, 102.

[102] African Union Peace and Security Council Communique', November 22, 2011 http://au.int/en/dp/ps/sites/default/files/299e%20CPS%20Communique%20LRA-eng-22-11-11_1.pdf (accessed 27 NOV 2011).

[103] Oghogho Obayuwana, "Nigeria to Contribute 16M Dollars Annually to AU Fund," BBC Monitoring International Reports, February 8, 2010, http://www.accessmylibrary.com/article-1G1-218520876/nigeria-contribute-16m-dollars.html (accessed March 14, 2012).

[104] Mike Denning, "A Prayer for Marie: Creating an Effective African Standby Force," *Parameters* (Winter 2004/2005), 102.

[105] Jakkie Cilliers, "The African Standby Force: An update on progress," Institute for Security Studies, ISS Paper 160, Pretoria/Tshwane, South Africa, March 2008, 7.

[106] Staff Sgt. Stefanie Torres, "Nigerians receive first C-130 after PDM," February 2, 2011, http://www.17af.usafe.af.mil/news/story.asp?is=123240766 (accessed January 18,2012).

[107] U.S. Africa Command Home Page, http://www.africom.mil/AboutAFRICOM.asp (accessed March 15, 2012).

[108] Linda M. Johnson, "U.S. Coast Guard Transfers High Endurance Cutters Hamilton and Chase to the Philippines and Nigeria," News from the U.S. Coast Guard Acquisition Directorate, May 2011, http://www.uscg.mil/acquisition/newsroom/pdf/cg9newsletterMay11.pdf (accessed March 21, 2012).

[109] United Nations, "Background Notes United Nations Peacekeeping," http://www.un.org/en/peacekeeping/documents/backgroundnote.pdf Ambassador Susan Rice, "Can the UN Keep the Peace," http://www.pbs.org/now/shows/520/index.html. (accessed march 15, 2012).

[110] Oghogho Obayuwana, "Nigeria to Contribute 16M Dollars Annually to AU Fund."

[111] Johnnie Carson, Assistant Secretary, Bureau of African Affairs, "U.S. Policy in sub-Saharan Africa, Before the House Committee on Foreign Affairs Subcommittee on Africa and Global Health, March 24, 2010 http://www.state.gov/p/af/rls/rm/2010/139002.htm (accessed March 14, 2012).